pop bonsai

pop bonsai

**Fun with Arranging
Small Trees
and Plants**

Lisa Tajima

Translated by **Kirsten McIvor**
Photographs by **Hisayoshi Osawa**

KODANSHA INTERNATIONAL
Tokyo • New York • London

NOTE

This book covers general techniques for growing and caring for plants, and the main bonsai techniques.

Over the centuries, people have studied ways to grow dwarf trees and use them to create forms with the same proportions as in nature. In the process they have developed a variety of techniques still indispensable for growing bonsai today.

These special techniques utilize the distinguishing features of each tree. But they can be difficult to master, and may not always achieve the desired outcome. Note also that the methods for growing and maintaining bonsai described here are general examples. Temperature and humidity vary by location, so choose methods for growing and maintaining each variety that suit the climate in your locality.

As you experiment with the techniques described in this book, make sure you first understand the special properties of your tree. Remember also to check its state of health, make sure you have chosen the best time of year to do the job, and proceed with caution. It is up to you to minimize stress on any trees you use.

All ceramics (except on pp. 62–63) were designed and made by Lisa Tajima

Jacket photo: Hisayoshi Osawa

Distributed in the United States by Kodansha America, Inc., 575 Lexington Avenue, New York, NY 10022, and in the United Kingdom and continental Europe by Kodansha Europe Ltd., Tavern Quay, Rope Street, London SE16 7TX.

Published by Kodansha International Ltd., 17-14 Otowa 1-chome, Bunkyo-ku, Tokyo 112-8652, and Kodansha America, Inc.

First edition, 2004
ISBN 4-7700-2980-2
04 05 06 07 08 09 10   10 9 8 7 6 5 4 3 2 1

www.thejapanpage.com

CONTENTS

pop bonsai

Introduction

Pop bonsai is great fun, and the fun is in trying out new things, applying bonsai techniques to a living tree to transform it into your own creation, and placing it in a container to display.

Pop bonsai is a concept that I came up with in 1999, after spending a number of months studying classical bonsai. Since my family never had any special interest in this hobby, let me explain how I came to take it up.

It all began the day my father collapsed suddenly on the golf course. He was rushed to the hospital with a brain hemorrhage, and finally left us after lying unconscious for a year.

My father was a chef and owner of a Japanese-style restaurant in a coastal town near Tokyo. Since the 1970s he had taken us on numerous trips to Hawaii, and whenever we were planning to visit the homes of friends there, he would go to the local market to find fresh seafood, and make dishes like sushi and tempura for everyone to share. When my father lost consciousness and we were no longer able to talk, I recalled again not only how many wonderful times we'd had together, but that he'd possessed a very Japanese skill in the ability to prepare the foods he made; this was a skill that had helped him communicate with people from all over the world.

Back then, I had no skills at all that could be described as distinctively "Japanese." My aim had always been to do something that involved using English, so on graduating from high school I traveled first to Britain and then to the United States, where I studied at Rockland Community College in the State University of New York. This was followed by work in Tokyo as a music journalist on radio and television, and writing music. But while I could speak English, I possessed not one skill to be proud of as a Japanese.

My father had fallen ill so suddenly that we as a family were at a complete loss. I think this is why one day on the way home from the hospital, my younger sister Nao-pu and I talked about going to live overseas if Dad died. After high school Nao-pu had studied in the U.K., earning her chef's license on returning to Japan, and helping out at the family restaurant along with our younger brother.

It was after this discussion with Nao-pu that it struck me: if things really did come to us moving overseas as a family, everyone but me—that is, my mother, brother and sister—would find it easy to get a working visa. They all had experience in the very Japanese world of "Japanese cooking," complete with licenses as proof of their professional qualifications. I had nothing of the kind. I wondered what I would do if we moved abroad, and decided that I too needed some sort of uniquely Japanese skill.

Even one would be a start. I called Mami, a friend since high school who had also studied overseas. She said that if she was me, she'd become a piano tuner, or do bonsai. (There's nothing particularly Japanese about piano tuning, it's just that Mami, who teaches music, feels that all the pianos she has played on in the U.S. have been badly out of tune.)

Her suggestion had a huge impact on me. The next day I bought a bonsai magazine at the local bookstore, called the number listed for the editorial department, and asked them to recommend a bonsai master to teach me. And so began my study of bonsai.

Eventually my father passed away, our plan to move overseas as a family proved nothing more than a distraction from the reality and stress of his illness, and my brother took over the restaurant and ran it with my mother and sister.

I found traditional bonsai a cool sort of pastime, an intriguing art form of great depth. However, the emphasis on tradition in any study of classical bonsai—doing things the way they have always been done—brings with it a long list of rules, leaving virtually no room for self-expression. So I began to study pottery on my own, and to plant bonsai that I had created in pots also of my own design. I figured if bonsai tended to be rule-bound, I'd express myself through the pots.

For fun I experimented with putting feet on one pot, then took it home for one of my bonsai. I was fascinated to find that this bonsai—until then a very sedentary thing—took on a far more dynamic look. There was something about the look that inspired me, and I was hooked. It wasn't long before the balcony of my apartment was crammed with bonsai with feet. Whenever I opened the window to look out at the balcony, my trees seemed about to walk off at any moment. While obviously still bonsai, they were clearly not bonsai of the traditional kind. Surely, I thought, there had to be a new name that would reflect this… So I dubbed them "pop bonsai."

As a student living in New York in the 1980s I was very familiar with pop art, and just loved popcorn, soda pop and pop music. To me the word "pop" came to be associated with having a great time doing things your own way.

Trying to think of a name for my style of bonsai, I opened a dictionary and looked up the word "pop." There I found pop also used in the phrase "pop off," meaning to die suddenly. How many times had I got up in the morning to find a bonsai had expired overnight? And my father had slipped so suddenly toward death—the main reason I took up bonsai. I was convinced therefore that taking "pop," a word encapsulating the idea of mass enjoyment, things that everyone likes, and of death, the ultimate destiny of us all, and using it to name my bonsai was not only a good idea in terms of the novelty of the sound and the arrangement of the letters, but a choice of deeper significance.

It was a name that came to me late one night over a glass of wine, and inspired me immediately. I should add that ever since I was little I have loved the Peanuts comic strip, and even now Snoopy and his friends have a special place in my heart. I also love the Nutcracker Suite, and clay animation TV programs and films. The more time goes by, the more I realize that with my background, tastes and preferences, it is no coincidence that I designed pots with feet, and thought of the name pop bonsai. It may well have been inevitable.

In due course, simply changing the pots while retaining traditional bonsai forms was not enough, and I began to come up with totally new styles, all the while studying more closely how trees function, and to give my bonsai their own messages, stories and names.

In the process I realized that pop bonsai is quite simply bonsai that ignores existing notions of what a bonsai ought to be. It is bonsai grown and displayed in ways that give free rein to our ideas, sensibilities and imagination. Some lovers of traditional bonsai may not be able to view my work as real "bonsai." But to me it represents a new, original and unique variation on an ancient art.

I hope that this book will inspire you to feel a deeper connection to trees and plants and a desire to create and care for your own pop bonsai.

A range of possible designs

KAZMAIER

HORST

Sixty Years
of
Photography

T&H

THE FRENCH LAUNDRY cookbook

THOMAS KELLER

ARTISAN

DIGITAL DIARIES

TASCHEN

VOGUE N. 539 · EDIZIONI CONDÉ NAST · LUGLIO 1995 · SPED. ABB. POST. / 50 · MI · LIRE 8.000

VOGUE N. 538 · EDIZIONI CONDÉ NAST · GIUGNO 1995 · SPED. ABB. POST. / 50 · MI · LIRE 8.000

VOGUE N. 537 · EDIZIONI CONDÉ NAST · MAGGIO 1995 · SPED. ABB. POST. / 50 · MI · LIRE 8.000

VOGUE N. 536 · EDIZIONI CONDÉ NAST · APRILE 1995 · SPED. ABB. POST. / 50 · MI · LIRE 8.000

VOGUE N. 549 · EDIZIONI CONDÉ NAST · MAGGIO 1996 · SPED. ABB. POST. / 50% · MI · LIRE 8.000

VOGUE N. 545 · EDIZIONI CONDÉ NAST · GENNAIO 1996 · SPED. ABB. POST. / 50% · MI · LIRE 8.000

LIVING WITH POP BONSAI

Live with pop bonsai, and every day you'll be reminded of how precious life is, and of the wonder of the seasons as they come around. Pop bonsai make great companions. But pop bonsai don't cry, or pester you for food. They just sit quietly and wait for you to come to them.

I always say, if you can learn to look after bonsai well, you can learn to love well too. Why? Because living with bonsai trees, which can't tell you what they want, requires you to be keenly aware of the needs of others. If you persist in working on a tree when the timing is inappropriate, the tree will probably die. If you neglect regular watering, or fail to notice damage caused by insects, your tree will find it hard to produce beautiful foliage. Keeping a tree indoors that normally grows best outside will stifle it and dramatically reduce its life span.

Living with pop bonsai can be compared to a romantic relationship or a close friendship. It requires a certain amount of care and attentiveness, but also provides a lot of satisfaction. If you fail to demonstrate through little everyday acts of kindness how much you care for the other person, and fail to notice subtle changes in them, eventually a gulf will form between you, and as it widens, love will wither and die. If you keep a tight rein on them and refuse to let go because you love them so much you want them near you all the time ... well, need I say more? Creating an environment that is pleasant for you and your companion alike takes some effort.

Buying a plant and simply displaying it is certainly better than having no greenery in your home or office at all. But if you can learn to prune the branches yourself, and use wire to bend that plant into a little pop bonsai of your own design, it will enhance your surroundings even more.

Trees are living things, and so are we. We do best existing side by side.

Pop bonsai can do more than bring a touch of nature into your world. It can change your quality of life and help you grow as a person.

The parts of a tree

When it comes to caring for trees, most important of course is to keep them alive. Knowing a few basic things about the structure of trees, and how each part of a tree functions, will keep your pop bonsai flourishing.

LEAVES

Leaves release moisture through transpiration, lowering the surrounding temperature to the level that the plant itself prefers. As they breathe, leaves use water and carbon dioxide to make carbohydrates and oxygen. The carbohydrates produced by photosynthesis are transported to the trunk, branches and roots to nourish the plant. The oxygen released is of course breathed by animals, including humans.

What else is needed for photosynthesis? Sunlight. Water sucked up by the roots is broken down into oxygen and hydrogen when tiny green bodies in the leaves called chloroplasts receive sunlight, the hydrogen joining with carbon dioxide to make carbohydrates.

Because bonsai trees are often displayed indoors, you may think they can grow indoors. However, the need for sunlight and the problem of keeping air flowing around the tree means that, except during dormant periods, it is extremely difficult to keep bonsai trees exclusively indoors. Leaves and sunlight are closely related, and some trees prefer half or full shade to direct sunlight. Knowing the environment preferred by your tree will help to increase its life span.

NUMBER OF LEAVES AND LIGHT

Having lots of leaves to make food is critical if your bonsai tree is to grow up strong.

This does not necessarily mean, however, the more leaves the better.

If a tree has dense foliage, some leaves will be shaded from sunlight, and air circulation will be poor, resulting in musty leaves prone to attack by pests and diseases. Reducing the number of leaves not only improves the appearance of your tree but is an important way of improving the environment in which the leaves grow.

CLOCKWISE FROM TOP LEFT: an unusual variegated Sargent juniper; Boulevard (a conifer); ivy; aronia; Trachelospermum with its attractive shiny foliage; the ginkgo, which also provides a spectacular autumn display; evergreen Sargent juniper; Japanese white pine; a dainty variegated boxwood; Glehnia littoralis and (in the middle) a maple.

TRUNK AND BRANCHES

The trunk and the branches together perform the important task of transporting water and nutrients. Water sucked up by the roots moves upward through the plant, while food produced by the leaves through photosynthesis travels downward via the trunk and branches. The trunk and branches are covered in a distinctive bark that varies from one tree to another. The black pine, for example, has a knobbly skin as if covered in rocks; the Indian lilac, smooth bark with white strips; and the Sargent juniper, a chocolate-colored bark. The distinctive texture and coloring of bark becomes increasingly obvious as trees age. The different styles of bonsai tree are created by the length and line of the trunk, and the number and length of the branches and which way they point.

TOP : the Indian lilac with its sensuously smooth pale trunk. Bottom: shaving to expose the white of the woody inner layer creates a striking contrast with the chocolate brown of the unshaved bark on this Sargent juniper. Left: the black pine is distinguished by the untamed look of its gnarled trunk.

SEEDS

Once the tree has flowered, and the stamen (male parts) and pistil (female parts) have mated and fertilization has occurred, the tree bears fruit, from which seeds emerge. Some trees will not produce fruit unless both a male and female tree are present, some bear fruit by themselves, while others have better results when two varieties of the same strain are cross-pollinated. If you want your tree to bear fruit, check with the person in the store that it does, before you buy. If they bear fruit, you can collect seeds from trees you already have. Alternatively, you can pick up seeds outdoors or in a park, or buy them at a garden store. Growing bonsai trees from seed is probably the cheapest way to enjoy bonsai. The reality, though, is that it does take time. I know of someone who planted a ginkgo nut she had found when she was twelve years old; she cultivated it carefully, and grew a wonderful bonsai over the course of seventy years. Most don't take that long, but growing an impressive tree will take a while. Of course, just like human babies, baby bonsai trees are certainly cute. If you are prepared to take the time to grow a bonsai tree from seed, make sure you enjoy each stage of the tree's growth. It is certainly a joy to know that you have watched a bonsai grow from nothing. I have one pop bonsai—a baby pine tree that germinated two years ago—which I sometimes move around the house with me, putting it next to the computer or setting it on the dinner table.

CLOCKWISE FROM TOP LEFT: acorns of the pasania found near my house; pumpkin seeds saved when cooking; store-bought Japanese white pine seeds; the unusual seeds of the Chinese moonseed (Sinomenium acutum); gardenia seed from my own tree; the sesame-like seeds of the Oriental bittersweet; and plum stones saved from dessert.

GERMINATION AND TEMPERATURE CHANGE

In regions with four distinct seasons, seeds that have spent winter outside in the ground sense that the cold winter has ended and spring has arrived by the change in temperature, and send up shoots.

So what about seeds that spend the winter indoors? They become accustomed to room temperature, so even if they are sown outside in spring, the difference between the temperature where they were stored and the temperature in the soil is minimal. This means the seeds themselves will not be able to differentiate between heat and cold, and may fail to germinate. For this reason, if you keep seeds in a heated room over winter, place them in the refrigerator to chill for about a week before you plan to plant them.

Thus, your seeds will move from a cold environment to a warm one, perceive the same temperature change as in nature, and have a better chance of germinating than if you simply sowed them without chilling first.

If you want to further improve the chances of germination, keep the seeds an extra two days in the refrigerator, soaked in water. Any seeds floating on the surface after two days will not germinate and can be discarded, while those that have sunk to the bottom can be taken out and sown.

Of course you can sow seeds in autumn too, just as in nature.

If you do get hold of any seeds in autumn, there is no reason not to sow them immediately.

SOWING SEEDS

The parts of a tree ● 31

1. Fill an unglazed pot or container with a drainage hole with soil.

2. Sow seeds at a suitable density according to their size. Give large seeds plenty of room, and sprinkle on smaller seeds.

   If seeds have any flesh on them, crush lightly and wash the flesh off carefully in water before planting.

3. Cover with a layer of soil around twice as thick as the size of the seed in spring, and five times the thickness in autumn. Water the seeds, taking care not to wash them away.

TIP

Until the seeds germinate, keep watering them. Do not let the soil on top dry out.

If you sowed your seeds in autumn, once the weather grows cold cover the container with a lid to protect them from frost.

Your seeds are unlikely to die even if the temperature drops below zero in midwinter and the ground freezes as long as they are not frostbitten. Once winter is over and spring is in the air, remove the lid.

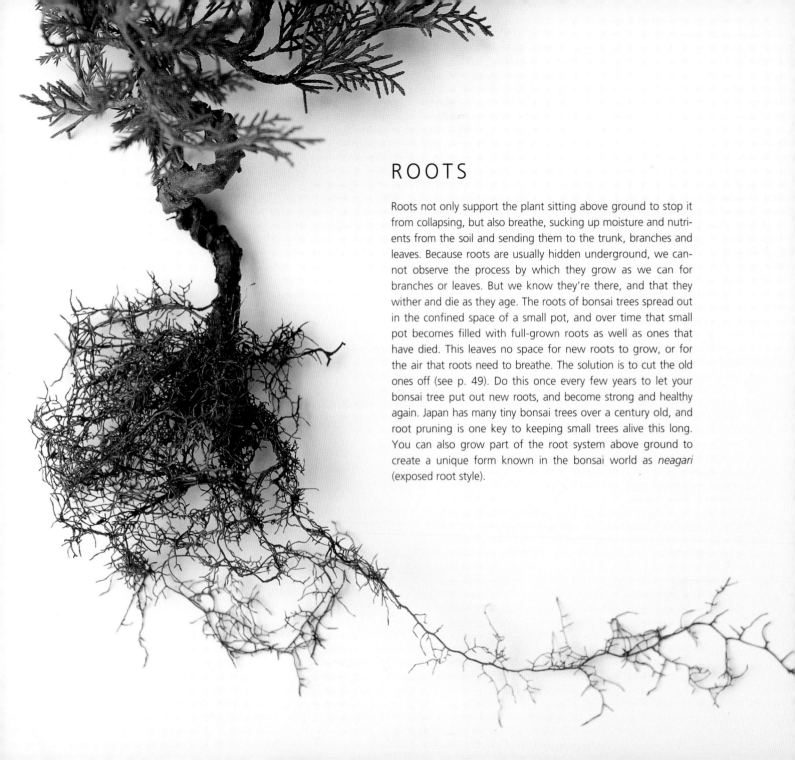

ROOTS

Roots not only support the plant sitting above ground to stop it from collapsing, but also breathe, sucking up moisture and nutrients from the soil and sending them to the trunk, branches and leaves. Because roots are usually hidden underground, we cannot observe the process by which they grow as we can for branches or leaves. But we know they're there, and that they wither and die as they age. The roots of bonsai trees spread out in the confined space of a small pot, and over time that small pot becomes filled with full-grown roots as well as ones that have died. This leaves no space for new roots to grow, or for the air that roots need to breathe. The solution is to cut the old ones off (see p. 49). Do this once every few years to let your bonsai tree put out new roots, and become strong and healthy again. Japan has many tiny bonsai trees over a century old, and root pruning is one key to keeping small trees alive this long. You can also grow part of the root system above ground to create a unique form known in the bonsai world as *neagari* (exposed root style).

EXPOSED ROOTS (*NEAGARI*)

To do this, leave thick, sturdy roots uncut, and expose several of these roots to grow above ground into a unique shape.

Use trees with roots that thicken easily. There are two different techniques for achieving a *neagari* effect. One is to raise the plant a little each time you repot, gradually bringing the thicker roots above the ground. For the other, cover the roots with a cylindrical plastic container with the bottom cut out, place a plant pot underneath, and fill both with soil (photo below). Grow for one or two years so that the roots extend straight down, then once the roots can stand upright without the plastic container, remove it and rinse off any excess soil to expose them. Generally, this second technique allows you to achieve a *neagari* effect more quickly, although it will depend on the tree.

Grow until the roots reach down into the pot underneath.

Making your own pop bonsai THE BASICS

Which branches to prune, and which to leave?

As you stand there with a tree in front of you, this is the first question that comes to mind. It should also be the most enjoyable part of creating a pop bonsai.

Because trees are living things, no two trees used as material for bonsai will be exactly alike. They may look the same, but they are all slightly different in some way. You can train their growth in similar ways, but the end result will never be two identical bonsai trees. Traditional bonsai are modeled on trees growing in nature, making it relatively simple to work out which branches to prune and which to leave, but no such rules apply in pop bonsai, so let your imagination run wild. Do remember, though, that leaves make food for the tree, and branches transport that food, so never prune your tree so drastically that most of the leaves and branches are lost.

First of all, stand back and take a good look at your tree. Then ask yourself some questions. Where does this tree grow? In a city park? Or deep in a forest? What is the temperature there? What would you find nearby? The sea? Or a bakery? Take that one small tree and make it the entire focus of your imagination. Things may come to mind as you look at it that at first glance have nothing to do with the tree. A bridge you often crossed as a child, a rainbow spotted in a gap between buildings, a lover who lives far away, your favorite food...

Naturally, if there is something you wish to express from the outset, proceed with this in mind. Project the image in your mind onto the tree in front of you. Then chop off any branches you think would be better gone, and shorten any you feel protrude too much, until the tree looks more like you imagined it. The important thing is to confine your cutting to branches and stalks. Leaves should not be cut with scissors: the cut surface will eventually turn brown, giving the tree a dirty appearance. With a plant that has a lot of fine leaves or needles, pull the leaves back to expose the branch before cutting. If while pruning you discover a particular feature of that tree you wish to highlight, do so. Keep your mind open to the possibilities, and

enjoy interacting with the tree. Smell the fragrance given off as you cut the branches; feel the texture of the leaves. As your creation begins to take shape, reduce the number of leaves in places with dense foliage so that light reaches all the leaves. To change the direction or flow of any branches, use wire to bend them into shape, and if the tree allows it, add a few more individual finishing touches, such as carving on the trunk, or peeling bark. And of course don't forget to take off any dead leaves.

SOME ORIGINAL POP BONSAI THEMES

BOOMERANG

Here I have used the trunk to depict the line formed by a boomerang that, if thrown skillfully, comes back to the thrower. This symbolizes the lesson that, over time, good deeds will be repaid by good, and bad by bad.

FOUNTAIN

Here the branches of the tree have been modeled on the continuous gushing of water. This was inspired by the hope that love and kindness spring eternal.

DRAGON

As the name suggests, this is patterned on the imaginary creature that summons clouds and makes it rain. Here my thoughts were of water, so essential for plants and animals, and the uncertainty caused by water shortages, always a problem somewhere in the world.

FERRIS WHEEL

A Ferris wheel, turning slowly and silently. From low to high, and then back to low again. Compare your life from birth to death to a Ferris wheel: where are you now?

NIAGARA FALLS

This design is modeled on the Niagara Falls with their spectacular and never-ending rush of water, and is for Sam, a dear friend born and raised near the Niagara Falls and now living in Manhattan.

SPIRAL

As the name suggests, I twisted the trunk of this tree into a spiral, reaching up into the sky. The idea is that if we keep looking upward as we grow, little by little, our wishes will one day come true.

POP BONSAI TOOLS

Three tools are essential for pop bonsai: scissors for pruning branches and roots, wire-cutters and tweezers.

These are all you need to create a small bonsai tree that fits easily in one hand. Choose tools that are comfortable to hold and use, allowing you to perform delicate tasks easily. For beginners, stainless steel tools are rust-resistant and easy to handle. All those discussed here are designed specifically for working on bonsai; however, gardening tools work just as well.

You will need a supply of aluminum wire. This is used to bend trunks and branches, and anchor trees in place. Special bonsai wire is also available. Try to keep a few different types of wire on hand, for tree trunks and branches of different thickness.

A small broom or brush for tidying up and a scoop for filling pots with soil are also handy, and will make these jobs more enjoyable.

FROM TOP: three tools—scissors for pruning branches and roots, wire-cutters and tweezers—with two types of wire.

Other essentials

SOIL

MOSS

AKADAMA SOIL
(SMALL LUMPS OF RED LOAM)

KETO SOIL
(SOIL WITH HIGH CLAY CONTENT)

SPHAGNUM MOSS

There are many types of soil, with more or less sand, clay and nutrients in them. Different plants do best with different kinds of soil, so be sure to ask, when you buy your seeds or plants, which kind is best.

MESH FOR THE BOTTOM OF THE POT

Mesh keeps insects out, and stops soil leaking from the bottom of the pot. Mesh designed specifically for this purpose is available, or you can cut up the mesh used in screen doors.

POT

This should have a hole in the bottom, and be made from a material that doesn't rust. Avoid pots with a base wider than the mouth: roots will grow to the shape of the pot, making them impossible to remove for repotting.

FROM LEFT: scoop (for soil), pick (for removing soil from roots, but pointed stick will do), knife and brush.

CHOOSING YOUR MATERIALS

The most important thing to remember when purchasing your tree is to pick a healthy one—after all, you'll be placing stress on it by doing things like pruning and bending the branches. Obviously, choose a tree free of pests and diseases. Study them before you buy, and choose a healthy, vigorous seedling. Any variety can be used for pop bonsai. Choose a tree readily available to you, that thrives in your local area.

The main things to remember when selecting a tree are as follows, depending on what you want to do with it:

IF YOU WANT TO CREATE A POP BONSAI USING JUST SCISSORS, choose a seedling with lots of bushy, intertwining leaves and branches, such as a boxwood or azalea. This will give you greater scope for shaping your tree.

IF YOU WANT TO CREATE A POP BONSAI BY WIRING A TREE AND BENDING ITS BRANCHES, choose a variety with supple branches, or a young specimen with a narrow trunk and branches, such as a pine or maple.

IF YOU WANT TO CREATE A POP BONSAI BY CARVING AND SHAVING A TREE, choose a hard, slow-growing, relatively sturdy type, like a juniper or an apricot.

IF YOU WANT TO USE TWIGS FROM THE TREE AS CUTTINGS FOR PROPAGATING MORE TREES, choose one that puts down roots readily and is easy to grow from cuttings, like a narrowleaf firethorn or rose.

DECIDUOUS AND EVERGREEN TREES

Plants are either deciduous or evergreen. In regions with four distinct seasons, deciduous trees lose all their leaves at the end of autumn, and put out new shoots in spring. In tropical regions, new shoots often appear soon after the leaves have fallen.

Evergreen trees have green foliage all the year around. Of course, evergreen leaves also fall off the tree after two to three years; but because a new leaf is already growing when this happens, the tree looks much the same all the time.

Deciduous trees make attractive bonsai because the viewer is able to enjoy the appearance of the tree as it changes with the seasons. In contrast, what makes evergreens attractive is exactly that—the fact that they are always green. Evergreens truly come into their own when deciduous trees have lost their leaves. When it comes to growing a pop bonsai, it isn't a matter of one or the other being easier to manage; use a tree that interests you, whether it is for the flowers or fruit, the beauty of the leaves, or some other reason.

WORKING ON YOUR TREE

You will do many things with your tree in the process of creating a pop bonsai, and afterward. Broadly speaking, work on trees falls into two categories. One is care essential to maintaining the health of the tree. The other is work that can be performed on the tree to enhance its individuality or attractiveness without affecting the health of the tree.

The first type is essential, while the second depends more on the personal preferences of the person creating the bonsai. Obviously, the more individual the shape, the more work of the second type is required. Applying yourself seriously to these jobs is only taking an enthusiasm for pop bonsai to its logical conclusion.

Here are the various things you can do with your tree, and the means required.

The b

USING SCISSORS

If we compare the process to, say, a beauty salon, then creating a pop bonsai with scissors alone is the equivalent of "just a cut." A cut forms the basis of any hairstyle, and regular cuts are essential to maintaining that style. The same applies in pop bonsai. When you take your scissors to a seedling to create a bonsai in your own special style, think about what the finished article will look like, and be prepared to make any cuts you need to achieve this look.

Of course, the results may not be quite what you hoped for the first time. Keep practicing, and hone your skills. Make the effort to give your tree a regular cut at the right time, to maintain its finished look. Because trees are living things, just as our hair grows, so over time do their leaves and branches. If you let leaves and branches grow unchecked, you will lose the style you've worked so hard to achieve. Trees grow especially fast when young, so generally you should aim to prune them once a year. As trees get older, their shoots don't grow as much; so if your tree was old to begin with, or has grown older over time, you only need to prune sections as they come to your attention.

ROUTINE PRUNING

If a tree is left to grow unchecked, shoots on the tips of branches will grow fast and most vigorously. If you let this happen, slowly but surely just the tips will grow long, destroying the balanced look of the tree. Routine pruning is therefore necessary. In a sense, this bonsai technique creates a kind of artificial emergency, to spur the lazy shoots into action. Take a close look at any branches exhibiting vigorous growth. You should find shoots spaced along them at roughly equal intervals. Usually, most of the shoots found between the shoot at the tip and the trunk are living, but if the one at the tip is growing very vigorously, those further down will tell themselves, "That guy'll bring us lots of food, so we can just let him get on with it. No need to strain ourselves," and refuse to grow. Some shoots will actually go to sleep!

Cut off that energetic shoot at the tip, and give those lazy shoots between tip and trunk a wake-up call. Once they realize what's happening they'll think, "Oh no! We'll starve if we stay like this! We've got to do something!" and will grow longer and start to form branches and leaves. Waking up the shoots near the trunk will allow the tree to regain its compact shape. Specifically, there will be more twigs; any new leaves that grow will usually be smaller than existing leaves; and the overall balance of the tree will improve.

WHEN TO PRUNE

REGIONS WITH FOUR DISTINCT SEASONS

As a general rule, prune in spring when new growth appears.

TROPICAL REGIONS

Simply prune when new shoots grow.

IF FLOWERS ARE THE FEATURE YOU WANT TO ENJOY

Generally speaking, it is better to prune branches and tidy the shape of the tree directly after it finishes flowering.

Trees tend to flower, though, in one of two ways, depending on the variety. The first category consists of trees that produce flowers in early summer from buds that grew the previous spring and have been on the tree over winter (plum trees, witch hazels, etc.). The second is trees that produce flowers the same year on the tips of branches that have grown that spring (roses, lilacs, etc.).

In the first case, if you miss the usual time for pruning, leave all the branches until next spring, so that you won't lose the part of branches that already have buds, which aren't easy to recognize.

In the second case, if you want to maintain the shape of the tree, shorten the branches once or twice (but no more) in very early spring.

One other rule: as soon as each flower has finished (except on fruit-bearing trees), pinch off the stalk.

WHEN FRUIT ARE THE FEATURE YOU WANT TO ENJOY

If fertilization has taken place when the tree is flowering and you want to watch it bear fruit, do not remove the flowers. Later, after seeing it in fruit, remember to snip off the stalk slightly below each fruit and remove it. This is important: if fruit are left on the tree for long periods, the tree will tire, and be less likely to flower the following year.

TIP

To keep your tree looking compact and small, continue to prune branches for the first couple of years. At the expense of flowers and fruit for a while, this will improve the tree's shape (and young trees don't produce much fruit anyway).

HOW DIFFERENT TREES GROW

Knowing how your tree grows is useful when you come to perform routine pruning.

Broadly speaking, trees grow in one of two ways. In the world of bonsai these are known as *tachisho* (standing) and *haisho* (creeping).

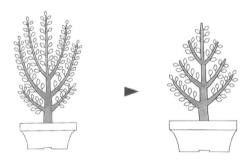

Tachisho—trees that stand upright easily, that are tall and grow vigorously upward.
WHAT HAPPENS: Branches at the top grow well; those farther down are weak and grow poorly.
SOLUTION: Cut branches at the top short, and allow those at the bottom to grow.

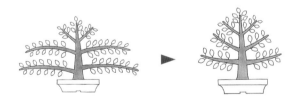

Haisho—trees that creep along the ground, i.e. the lower section spreads out horizontally, giving the tree a triangular shape.
WHAT HAPPENS: Branches at the top grow poorly; those at the bottom spread rapidly sideways.
SOLUTION: Cut bottom branches short, and allow those at the top to grow.

If you choose a seedling with small leaves for your pop bonsai, a good idea is to keep the tree short and its overall shape and contours compact. Doing this you'll find even a spindly trunk will appear thick and sturdy ... a little pop bonsai magic to make a little tree look like a big one! And remember big trees don't have branches within our reach, so remove any branches growing lower down to expose the trunk.

CUTTING FOR STYLE

TIP

Always cut branches or stalks. If you cut across leaves with scissors, the cut surface will eventually turn brown, detracting from the tree's appearance.

If any sections have thick layers of foliage, thin to allow all leaves access to light.

If the trunk and/or branches of your seedling are covered in foliage, simply stripping off all the leaves except those on the very tips will draw attention to the trunk and branches, giving the tree a totally different, dramatic look. It's a very simple but effective technique, and one of my favorites. With only the leaves at the tips remaining, it is easy to wire any branches for bending. Shaping a tree by removing leaves in this way is a fundamental technique very handy for creating pop bonsai in your own style.

CUTTINGS (*SASHIKI*)

Branches cut during shaping or routine pruning can be planted to put down roots and supply new seedlings. This can be done from when new growth first appears through autumn.

1. Immerse the cut branch in a container of water soon after cutting, and soak for at least an hour to absorb water.

2. If the branch has a lot of foliage, nutrition will be diverted to the leaves, making for poor root growth. So if your branch is a thin one with a dense covering of foliage, remove all the leaves from about the bottom half. If the branch has small to mid-size leaves, leave 2-4 at the top and take off all the lower ones. If the branch has very large leaves (about 4 inches in diameter), again, leave 2-4 on the branch and remove the others, then use scissors to cut the remaining leaves in half; these leaves will die but the roots will do well and new shoots will appear. Always remove any flower buds.

3. Fill an unglazed pot with the best soil for its plant, and push the cutting in the soil.

4. Keep away from direct sunlight and strong winds, remembering to water. When new shoots appear, move to a location that receives sun. Note that cuttings may still fail to take root even if all these steps are followed, depending on the type of tree and timing of the operation.

CUTTINGS

3 YEARS LATER

7 YEARS LATER

DEFOLIATION (*HAGARI*)

What make bonsai trees unique are their compact size and well-balanced appearance, and in the world of bonsai there are numerous techniques for keeping leaves small. One of these is *hagari* or defoliation. This involves cutting off any leaves too large for the thickness or length of the trunk and branches, allowing new shoots to appear, to obtain small leaves that match the trunk and branches.

If the region you live in is one with four distinct seasons, deciduous trees will usually only lose their leaves once a year. If any part of your tree is trimmed of leaves in this way, however, the tree is effectively losing its leaves twice in one year, which places considerable strain on the plant; so there is no need to perform this operation if it isn't really required. If you do decide to defoliate the tree, for evergreens other than conifers, cut off all the leaves before the new shoots start to grow out. This way, all new leaves that grow will be the same size, improving the appearance of the tree. For deciduous trees, as soon as new shoots grow and the leaves open out completely, select any leaves that are too big and remove them.

ROOT PRUNING (*NEKIRI*)

Roots have many functions, and giving them good care is extremely important (see p. 32). Generally they are pruned once every two years or so—around spring as the weather warms up or autumn as the weather grows cooler in seasonal regions; and in tropical regions where trees are active all the year around, when new shoots start to appear. Never prune roots at very hot or very cold times of the year. Use a pair of sharp scissors to prune roots, either bonsai or gardening scissors, cutting the thicker, longer roots, and leaving the thinner, shorter ones untouched.

1. Remove tree from pot. If the tree won't come out easily, press drainage hole in the base of the pot to remove it.

2. Use a metal pick or stick with a narrow tip to untangle the roots, removing any old soil. Do this carefully to avoid damaging the more delicate roots. There is no need to remove every speck of old soil.

3. Prune roots, starting with the thickest and longest, cutting about one-third of their length. Leave thinner, shorter roots.

4. Place mesh in bottom of pot and fix with wire, add a loose covering of fresh soil, position tree at the desired angle, then add more soil.

5. Poke the stick into the soil, working soil in to ensure it reaches between the roots. If necessary add more soil.

6. Pass a piece of rustproof wire with the tip cut on a diagonal up through the hole in the base of the pot to the surface of the soil. Bend end of wire and pull from below to fix tree in place. Take the wire sticking out of the bottom and bend it in one direction, leaving a suitable length, and cut off the rest. If the tree is not firmly anchored in this one place, repeat several times until it is.

    Immerse in water immediately. Pour on water evenly, or place pot in a bucket of water base first, and soak well until water rises to the surface of the soil.

1

2

3

4

5

6

USING WIRE

Wrap wire artfully around the trunk or branches, to bend them. Wire allows you to do things that basic cutting with scissors or shears alone doesn't. Returning to our beauty salon theme, this job of giving the trunk or branches of your tree a new kind of flow or dynamism could be called a "perm." Wiring is certainly not essential, but personally I find it one of the most satisfying aspects of pop bonsai. Be very careful not to snap the trunk or branches while bending them.

THINGS TO KNOW

Choose wire of a suitable gauge for the trunk or branch in question. Often it's best to use wire that seems just a little thick, as this will hold the trunk or branch securely. If winding one piece of wire around the trunk or branch fails to bend it, wind another piece of the same thickness around it in the same direction, so the two lengths of wire are parallel.

Make sure the wire sits snugly against the surface of the tree. If it isn't wound tightly enough, the trunk or branch won't stay in place; if wound too tightly, it may cut into the surface of the tree, damaging it.

The idea is simply to bend the trunk or branch, so there is no point in coiling wire closely around it. The wire should loop around the trunk or branch at moderate intervals.

When wiring a trunk or branches, leave a reasonable space when winding and make sure the wire sits snugly against the tree, as shown on the far left. Avoid coiling the wire around and around without gaps as in the next sample. When using two pieces of wire, wind the second piece onto the tree parallel to the first, in the same direction. Intersecting wires like those on the far right will spoil the appearance of your tree.

BEFORE BENDING

AFTER BENDING

To bend a tree trunk or branch, use both hands to grip the part you wish to bend, keep your fingers firmly together, and bend slowly a little at a time (left). Never try to bend by pulling on leaves or applying excess force (right).

Remove wire by snipping off in short segments using wire-cutters. Watch out for flying pieces of wire, and if necessary wear goggles or some other form of eye protection.

TREES SUITABLE FOR WIRING

Choose flexible trees with pliant branches that bend when grasped lightly between your fingers. Flexibility has more to do with the nature of the tree than thickness. There are some trees that start life with a rigid trunk and branches, and others that grow more rigid with age. Forcing a rigid trunk or branch to bend will only break it, so when selecting seedlings with wiring in mind, avoid this kind of tree.

HOW LONG TO KEEP YOUR TREE WIRED

Generally speaking, trees are wired for approximately two months to two years. Because the aim is to hold the trunk or branch in position until it becomes accustomed to its new "pose," the wire is removed once this is done. Over time the trunk or branch will grow wider and the wire will start to cut into the tree, so observe the tree closely and remove the wire before this happens. If the trunk or branch does not appear to be firmly bent in place even after the wire starts to cut in, remove the wire and redo with new wire. Use wire-cutters to cut away the wire in suitable places, rather than unwinding, to avoid damaging the tree.

USING A KNIFE

Carving and shaving your tree: on our list of beauty salon services these tasks, which involve working on your tree using a knife to create contrasting colors and textures, are the equivalent of "coloring." Like coloring your hair, they are not essential, but a great optional extra.

Just why has this technique been in bonsai for so long? The answer lies in nature itself. Take a good look at a tree growing in its natural environment. You will see dead branches here and there, and places where part of the bark has peeled off the trunk, exposing the inner layer known as the xylem, i.e. the woody part of the tree. Such phenomena occur for a variety of reasons, including heavy snowfall, lightning, strong winds and man-made tampering. But they also remind us of the powerful life force that trees possess, which keeps them alive despite the damage. The practice of carving and shaving bark from bonsai trees seems to have arisen out of a desire to reproduce the appearance of trees in nature. There is nothing particularly difficult about these techniques, so apply them in ways that reflect your own aesthetic sense, to create a pop bonsai that is truly unique.

SHAVING AND CARVING YOUR TREE

New shoots will not grow from parts of a tree that have been carved or had the bark peeled off. Sections stripped of bark are also more prone to decay than those covered in bark, so harder, denser trees that grow slowly and take a long time to thicken are more suitable for shaving or carving than softer, less dense trees that thicken faster.

PEELING BARK FROM THIN BRANCHES

1. Grip base of branch lightly with scissors, and score right around the circumference.

2. Cut off all leaves.

3. Grip the branch with pliers and gently crush it all over. This will make it easier to separate the surface bark from the woody section in the middle.

4. Use your fingers to pick off bark. If the bark won't peel off, try grasping the branch with the pliers and applying pressure again.

Whittle the bark off thick branches in much the same way as you would sharpen a pencil.

CARVING

Food for the tree is transported through the bark, so the bark must remain connected vertically. When carving the trunk of a tree, never sever the bark through its entire circumference.

Carve carefully a little at a time on parts of the trunk, using a knife or whatever else you find easy to use. Be careful how deeply you carve: too deep and you may penetrate parts that carry water, with serious consequences for the life of the tree.

LAYERING (*TORIKI*)

A knife can also be used to shorten a tree, and to create multiple shorter trees from one tall tree. If a small tree of the right size is unavailable, this method will allow you to produce your own substitutes.

Layering involves removing bark from the entire circumference of the trunk about halfway up, and growing new roots from this location. The same can also be done along branches, or to trees growing in the garden. Generally, the most suitable time to layer is just before new shoots appear. Note that this method may not always result in roots.

BEFORE STARTING

Decide where you would like the tree to grow roots, and make a cut right around the trunk at this location. Then make another cut, again around the entire circumference of the trunk, at a point twice the diameter of the trunk below this.

1. Insert the knife vertically and peel off the bark. Roots will not grow if even a tiny amount of light green bark remains, so whittle away bark completely until the xylem appears.

2. Cover trunk in plastic, securing it with twine or the like below the cuts. Cover the cuts with a generous layer of sphagnum moss that has been wet thoroughly. The moss functions as a soil substitute, so failure to use enough will reduce the likelihood of roots growing.

3. Fasten the plastic at the top as well. Water the tree as you would normally, and wait for roots to grow. When the sphagnum moss dries out, unfasten the top of the plastic and add plenty of water, then close up again. Once the roots grow you will be able to monitor them through the plastic.

TWO TO THREE MONTHS LATER

When they have grown sufficiently, cut off just below the new roots, transfer with the sphagnum moss to a pot containing soil, and propagate for around a year.

THE FOLLOWING SPRING

Remove once roots have grown thick and sturdy, take out all the sphagnum moss, being careful not to damage roots, and replant in a pot.

1

2

3

Making your own pop bonsai
COMBINING ELEMENTS

Bringing trees and ideas together.
Ten different people will create ten
different pop bonsai, and display
them in at least ten different ways.
You too should use your imagination to experiment.

POTS

Planting a tree in a different pot can completely alter the image it projects.

If trees were humans, pots would be their clothing. Just as you and I choose what to wear according to our mood that day, who we expect to meet, and where we are going, your pop bonsai can have "outfits" for different settings and occasions. Exercise a little ingenuity when choosing a pot, and add extra "pop" to your bonsai.

COVERING THE POT

Pots used to plant trees directly must have a hole in the base, and not be prone to rust. They should also retain moisture, so unglazed or ceramic pots are best. This does, however, limit your selection a little, so one pop bonsai idea is to cover the pot in some way, extending the range of looks you can achieve.

To display your tree in a container made from a material you want to keep dry, such as paper or cloth, first put the pot in a close-fitting container made of plastic or glass, without a hole in the base. Something as simple as placing the pot on an aluminum can will also give your creation a novel, "pop" appearance, and prevent any water left in the pot from spilling on the tablecloth.

ANOTHER IDEA
Fold and seal a clear plastic bag so that one end is peaked, like a pyramid. Cut a small round opening for the tree. (See p. 15)

STUDYING DIFFERENT ANGLES FOR PLANTING

There is no need to keep planting a tree at the same angle.

Tipping the tree slightly to the left or right, or far back or forward, can give it a more dramatic appearance, and increase the range of styles available to you.

So when you are trying to come up with new ideas, don't forget to take another look at the angle of your tree.

ORDINARY ANGLE

NEW ANGLE

ROCKS AND STONES

Pop bonsai can also be grown on rocks and stones. A tree growing on a rock is a unique and intriguing sight. Try placing your bonsai on a favorite rock of yours. Avoid stones picked up near the sea, since these may contain a lot of salt. Instead use those found in the hills, or by rivers. The hardness is not important. Pumice is good, as is lava rock. You can use stones of different shapes, or combinations of stones, arranged at different angles, to create a whole host of different rocky bonsai.

Because rocks and stones absorb heat readily and lose moisture quickly, be sure to water the tree more often at hotter times of the year.

PLACING A TREE ON A ROCK BASE

BEFORE STARTING

Use a drill or similar tool to make shallow holes in two to four places on the rock or stone, and insert a short wood screw made from stainless steel or other rustproof material in each hole. Wind a piece of wire, again of a rustproof material, around the screws to fix the tree in place. For soft, thin stones, if you can drill holes right through the stone without breaking it, make two to four holes and pass a piece of rustproof wire through these to keep the tree in place.

IF THE ROCK OR STONE IS TOO HARD TO DRILL EVEN SHALLOW HOLES

Use instant adhesive to attach a piece of wire made from rustproof material firmly to the rock or stone. Spread on some waterproof putty or similar stuff (of the type used to repair bathtubs, i.e. that won't lose its strength when wet), to ensure the wire is attached properly, then fix the tree in position once the putty is completely dry.

IF THE ROCK OR STONE HAS BUMPS OR HOLLOWS

Wrap wire around the rock or stone utilizing any bumps or hollows, and if necessary fix in place using instant adhesive. If the wire is still not firmly attached to the rock, top with waterproof putty to reinforce before fixing the tree in place.

IF YOU DON'T MIND THE WIRE BEING VISIBLE, simply wrap rustproof wire around the rock as
many times as necessary to hold the rock or stone and tree firmly in place.

1. Combine soil with high clay content and Akadama soil (small lumps of red loam) at a ratio of 7:3 and mix well. If the mixture appears a little dry, add water until the soil feels slightly firmer than your earlobe.

1

2. Fix wire to the rock or stone using a suitable method (see above). Attach at least two strands of wire, positioning them so that they will intersect in the location you wish to place the tree.

3. With the wires hanging loose, place a thin layer of clay-like soil on the part of the rock or stone on which you wish to place the tree.

4. Place tree on top, add more soil of the same consistency, and press down so that rock, tree and soil adhere firmly to each other.

5. Cross strands of wire over the rock so that they intersect, and fix tree in place by pushing them down into the dirt. If you have some moss to use as decoration, push it onto the surface here and there with tweezers.

Note: I've used thick wire here, to make the illustrations easier to understand. But it's much better to work with thinner wire.

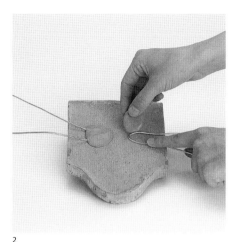

2

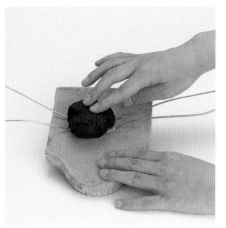

3

4

5

MOSS

There are said to be over twenty thousand varieties of moss in the world. Fluffy green carpet moss looks beautiful just the way it is, or can be made into "moss balls" by planting it here and there in soil that has been formed into a ball. Moss proliferates through spores, and you can grow more moss by cutting off the tips and spreading them around.

Growing moss in conditions close to those of its natural environment is the secret to obtaining long-lasting moss of good color. So when you gather moss, take detailed notes about where the moss was growing: whether it was in full sun, half-shade or full shade, and whether the place was wet or dry.

Regardless of whether you have any moss, using soil of a clay-like consistency to shape the roots of the plant into a "bonsai ball" is a convenient way of arranging your tree easily in any kind of pot. This technique has all sorts of practical applications, and can also be used for foliage plants. If green moss is difficult to obtain, even just wrapping the ball in wet sphagnum moss will give the plant an interesting appearance. With or without moss, if the roots are formed into a ball, the plant can be grown as is.

MAKING A BONSAI BALL

1. Chop up some sphagnum moss roughly. Make a mixture of soil with high clay content, Akadama soil and sphagnum moss in a ratio of 5:2.5:2.5, and knead together  thoroughly. If the mixture requires moisture, add water until it reaches a consistency slightly firmer than your earlobe.

2. Place this mixture a little at a time on the roots of your bonsai tree, having first lightly removed the old soil, and squeeze to form a ball, making sure that the mixture reaches between the roots. When all the roots are hidden, work into your desired shape, keeping in mind how you want to arrange the tree.

3. Wind cotton thread around the surface. Do this meticulously, winding the thread at decent intervals, not just from one direction, but both vertically and horizontally. The aim is simply to stop the soil from crumbling, so there is no need to cover the soil surface completely. If you have green moss, use tweezers to plant it on the surface.

1

2

3

To give the roots extra moisture and to preserve the shape, after covering with the soil mixture and before winding the cotton thread over the surface, cover the ball with wet sphagnum moss, then wind the thread around on top. The same technique can be used with sheets of green moss.

The next step is to water the ball just as you would a tree planted in a pot. If the water fails to penetrate completely, the plant will suffer from lack of moisture. To avoid this, from time to time place it in a bucket of water and gently knead the balled section to ensure that water soaks right in. If the tree still appears in poor condition, cut the thread and break up the ball early, lightly remove the hardened soil, return tree to a plant pot and try growing in a regular environment.

GROWING MOSS

1. Prepare a plant pot of soil.

2. Cut off tips of moss and sow flat on surface of the soil, pressing down with your fingers.

3. Until temporary roots appear, water carefully, to stop moss from washing away.
   The moss you sowed will eventually die off, but the spores dispersed from it will sprout new shoots, which will grow into moss.

Generally, allow 2–3 months for the new moss to grow.

STORING MOSS

If moss is left for long periods in a badly ventilated room, it may go moldy and rot. When making a bonsai solely of moss, the same applies as for bonsai trees: avoid leaving indoors for more than two days.

GROUP PLANTING

I recommend planting several of the same variety of tree in the same pot. This makes tasks like root pruning and repotting easier, and avoids shortening the life of the tree unnecessarily. If you really do wish to combine different varieties in the same pot, view it as a temporary arrangement, perhaps as a table decoration for a special occasion, and when you've finished displaying the bonsai, return the trees to different pots. Growing different varieties in the same pot for any length of time results in the roots becoming entwined, and the tree with the fastest-growing roots filling up the pot, stunting the growth of the other trees and reducing their life spans. There are many ways to create interesting group plantings using just one type of tree.

GROUP PLANTING (*YOSE-UE*)

For group plantings, always use a container with a hole in the base. The material should be something that will not rust or rot. Alternatives include kitchen utensils such as sieves or plastic boxes with mesh bottoms. More space will give more options for your group planting. If your container is deep, fill with a suitable quantity of soil, place the trees in the desired location, then add more soil to fill in the gaps, and the trees should stay in position. If the container is shallow, you may not be able to fix the trees with soil alone, so do the following:

BEFORE STARTING

Prepare small balls of soil of high clay-like consistency (see p. 68).
Use wire to fix the mesh over hole in base of pot (see p. 49).

1. Position one tree in the pot, and surround roots with balls of the same soil and push them down to fix the roots in place.

2. Position another tree in the pot, and surround roots with balls of soil in the same way to fix them in place. Repeat for all the trees you wish to plant together.

3. Fill remaining space in the pot with soil. Pour on water evenly, or place the pot in a bucket of water base first, and soak well until the surface of the soil is thoroughly wet.

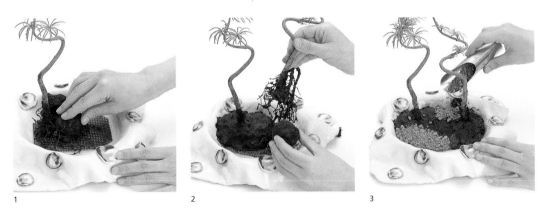

1   2   3

TIP

If the tree will still not stay in place, insert a piece of rustproof wire up through the hole in the base of the container and use this to complete the job. After a while, the tree will put out fine roots through the soil to stabilize it naturally.

RAFT STYLE (*IKADABUKI*)

This technique involves cutting all the branches off one side of a single tree, and planting the tree with the trunk lying down to give the impression of several small trees growing together. In nature too, the branches of a tree that has fallen over, after being struck by lightning, for example, may continue to live in this form. This operation should be performed around spring in seasonal areas, just as the weather starts to get warmer, and in tropical areas when new growth starts to appear.

1. Cut all branches off one side of the tree. Do the opposite to the roots, cutting off those on the side still with branches.

2. Lay the tree down in a pot of soil, pass wire up through the hole in the base, and fix in place. If this isn't enough, use pieces of U-shaped wire (see illust. below).
   Over time, roots will grow from the trunk. Once these have grown and stabilized, you can wire the sections that were formerly branches to shape them, creating even more intriguing landscapes.

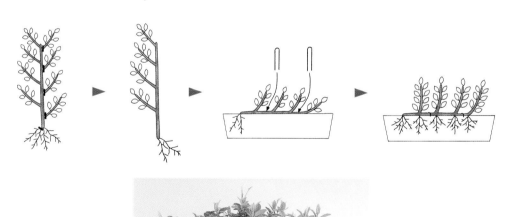

ABOUT 10 YEARS LATER

Special displays

Experiment with arranging and displaying your original bonsai to suit any occasion—a seasonal event, a birthday, an anniversary or a party for friends. Combine with cut flowers or candles, perhaps a card with a message, or anything else handy. When it comes to displaying your pop bonsai, the sky's the limit. A bonsai arranged in this way will convey the message you want to send, bring enjoyment to your guests, and be a great conversation piece.

BIRTHDAYS

After going to all that trouble to make your pop bonsai, why not let it join in the party? Eggshells from cooking or the scooped-out skins of fruit make great pots. Keeping a plant growing in a hollowed fruit is difficult, but gently pressing a layer of moss onto the soil lets you enjoy your arrangement for several days. Giving a pop bonsai is also the perfect way to thank those who come to share the event.

NEW YEAR'S

Pop bonsai of your own creation make an excellent festive season display in any culture. One New Year's in Japan, I displayed a pop bonsai growing on a flat stone on a stand, alongside some of my own calligraphy, some charcoal (believed to have a purifying effect on the air) made by burning bamboo chopsticks, and a small paper screen, both bought in Kyoto.

Think about what you can display with a particular tree, and you'll soon come up with any number of interesting ideas. For Halloween, though, nothing beats a pumpkin! To add some color, I used FIMO (a German plasticine that can be baked in the oven) to make a couple of grinning pumpkins and a "fallen angel" of my own design, with a handful of small chestnuts for company. Placing the decoration on a wooden board completed the effect, showing off the arrangement to best advantage.

History of bonsai

Bonsai has a long history and, according to one theory, was brought to Japan from China around 1200 years ago. Scrolls painted in the Heian period depict box garden-like arrangements with plants growing on trays, while a potted tree with branches that have been bent appears in *Tsurezuregusa* written by the essayist Yoshida Kenko (1282–1350), showing that people already appreciated something resembling bonsai by this time.

The most famous bonsai enthusiast in Japanese history was Iemitsu, the third Tokugawa shogun of the Edo period (1603–1867). Incredibly, a pine tree believed to have been owned by Iemitsu is still alive and thriving in Japan some 300 years later. This tree is reputed to have been a sizeable specimen even in Iemitsu's day, which suggests it may in fact be around 500 years old.

In the Meiji period (1868–1912), knowledge of bonsai techniques, after being passed on and shared among the residents of the Imperial Palace, eventually spread to people in political and financial circles, and then to ordinary citizens, with the publication of books on the subject and articles in newspapers. By this time, bonsai exhibitions were also being held.

As Japan enters the 21st century, the concept of less formal bonsai at a more accessible price is gaining ground among younger people, alongside more traditional bonsai.

Care and maintenance

LOCATION

Set up a suitable shelf or similar construction in your garden or on your balcony, as a home for your pop bonsai.

Trees are designed to live outdoors, so keep bonsai trees outside most of the time. Although humans don't really sense it, the air indoors is still, and if a tree is left inside for a long period its water will grow stagnant, the soil will rot, as will the roots, and the tree will die. Generally, bonsai trees can be kept indoors without any harm for up to two days or so. If you display your tree for a couple of days indoors, be sure to leave it out in your garden or on the balcony for at least three days after that.

During summer (throughout the year in tropical areas), concrete floors reach surprisingly high temperatures due to the heat radiating off them, so never place your bonsai directly on the floor.

In terms of light, most important for bonsai trees is to receive sun in the morning. In contrast, be extremely wary of locations that receive a lot of sun in the afternoon. During summer, in particular—and throughout the year in tropical areas—use a sunshade or similar device to shield the tree, otherwise your bonsai will run the risk of scorched leaves.

You may be able to raise a bonsai tree indoors if the location has both light and natural ventilation, such as a sunroom or a room with French windows. Overnight dew will, however, add luster to your bonsai's leaves, so provided it isn't cold try to put the tree outside occasionally, even if only at night.

INDOOR DISPLAY

Position your tree somewhere safe and secure, out of reach of pets and small children, avoiding locations in the direct path of air currents from heaters or air conditioners.

A WINTER HOME FOR YOUR BONSAI

In areas with four distinct seasons: if it snows in winter or the temperature falls below freezing point, move your bonsai tree indoors for the cold period, but only to a place just warm enough to stop it from freezing. There is no need to warm the tree by artificial means. Most trees are dormant during the winter, like animals that go into hibernation, and consequently don't require much light, although this does depend on the type of tree. Once you have moved your tree to a warmer location, remember to water it when the surface of the soil dries out. But beware: over-watering a tree kept inside for winter is not good for it.

In winter, even in areas where the temperature does not fall below freezing, make an effort to shelter plants that are vulnerable to cold winds. A simple way to do this on your balcony is to keep the bonsai enclosed on a shelf or under some kind of stand, made from a material that doesn't need to be kept dry; cover it with a thickish sheet of clear plastic, and weigh the sheet down with a stone to prevent it from blowing away. On fine days, lift the sheet during the day and expose the tree to the breeze.

An alternative is to use a polystyrene carton with drainage holes in the bottom.

DURING STRONG WINDS

If strong winds such as typhoon conditions are forecast, bring trees inside to shelter. If high winds are a regular occurrence in your area, use a sturdy elasticized cord or similar item to anchor pots to the shelf, to stop trees from falling and prevent branches from breaking.

FERTILIZER

Any fertilizer used widely in gardening or horticulture should be suitable. Do be careful, though, not to overdo it. Giving a plant in poor condition large doses of fertilizer is like force-feeding high-calorie foods to a person recovering from illness: it will have the opposite effect to that desired. Never fertilize immediately after repotting, or when a plant is in flower, or when it is in a weakened state, or in midsummer or midwinter. Find out the best time to fertilize that particular plant, and do so in appropriate quantities.

PROTECTING YOUR TREE FROM PESTS AND DISEASES

Placing a small amount of Ortran in a corner of the pot around the time new shoots are starting to grow will help keep insects at bay. Insects and bacteria are most active from spring through autumn. The best defense is to make it a habit when watering to check the tree for any signs of leaves being eaten, insects on the back of leaves or on the trunk and branches, or any parts that have changed color, allowing you to identify problems quickly. Left undiscovered, there is a serious risk of damage spreading to other trees nearby. If your tree is damaged by insects or disease, ask for advice at a specialist store, and treat the tree with something appropriate.

WATERING

It's difficult to make any generalizations about watering: depending on factors such as temperature and humidity, you may only need to water once a day, or you may need to do it twice or, conversely, just once every two days. The most important thing is to keep the surface of the soil moist. This does not mean that all is well provided the surface soil is damp. If you simply wet the surface using a mister, not only will moisture fail to reach the tips of the roots, but the air the roots need won't permeate the soil. So use a watering can or hose (with a spray attachment or something similar so that the water comes out as a mild shower) to keep your tree well watered. If you are raising your bonsai tree where it isn't practical to spray water around, as in a city office, an alternative is to pick the pot up and lower it into a bowl of water, allowing water to be absorbed through the hole in the base of the pot, and remove it when sufficient water has risen to the surface of the soil.

CARE AT HOT TIMES OF THE YEAR

When the weather is hot, water evaporates faster, and ideally trees should be watered several times a day. But if you are busy or out of the house, this is not always possible. A suggestion for those who do lead busy lives is to make up a fairly large container of soil with a hole in the bottom, bury the pot with the bonsai tree in this, and water the whole of the container thoroughly every day. This will keep moisture in the pot at a suitable level for a certain period of time, avoiding drying out much more effectively than if the smaller pot was standing on its own.

WATERING IN WINTER

Water whenever the surface of the soil dries out. Although it depends how dry the soil gets, take special care not to over-water bonsai kept indoors.

IF YOU ARE ABSENT FROM HOME FOR LONG PERIODS, OR FIND DAILY WATERING A CHORE
An automated sprinkler system is handy for this. Simply set the timer, and a fixed volume of water will be sprinkled automatically. Sprinkler systems are available wherever gardening accessories are sold. Choose one suitable for the location.

THE RELATIONSHIP BETWEEN WATER AND ROOTS

While a bonsai tree may die through lack of water, it is fairly rare for a tree to die from over-watering. It is important, however, to give your tree fresh water regularly, and allow any excess to drain out of the pot. If old, brackish water is left in a pot saucer that is too deep, and the pot soaks in this for months on end, you will indeed succeed in killing your bonsai tree. Generally speaking, when moisture gets scarce, the roots of the plant will grow longer, as if stretching out their hands in search of water to satisfy their thirst. Left soaking in water, the roots will certainly not grow; on the contrary, they will rot. It is absolutely essential not to let this happen.

List of trees and plants used

Acknowledgments

I would like to dedicate this book to my father, who is no longer with us. Papa, I can never give you a big hug again, but I feel you're always by my side. Thanks also to my sister Nao-pu and brother Jun-pu, and to Mama. I love you, forever.

Pop Bonsai could not have been completed without the superb technical skills and style sense of my photographer, Hisayoshi Osawa. Thank you for all those ingenious tricks and ideas; I'll never forget the time spent in your studio. And to your assistant Kanno-kun, thanks as well. I hope you succeed in finding your own special path in life.

A huge thank-you to everyone who has supported me through this project. I'm afraid there are too many of you to name here: friends, fans, staff, those of you from the world of traditional bonsai. Knowing you all has sustained me and helped make me what I am today.

On a personal and spiritual level I'd also like to thank Linkin Park and the Mad Capsule Markets. The sounds you create and your honest approach to music give me courage, strength and hope.

To my faithful companions Miyabow, Kechang, Kazu-p, Ta-chang, Udopan, Micky and Mu-chang: thank you for keeping me relaxed and happy.

A word also to the staff at Kodansha International: Editor-in-Chief Tetsuo Kuramochi, editors Takayo Tachikawa and Nobuko Tadai, and designer Kazuhiko Miki, for developing this book project and offering so many valuable suggestions. Thanks as well to translator Kirsten McIvor, for her patience with the numerous changes and additions to the text.

And last but not least, thanks to you the reader for buying *Pop Bonsai*. If this book inspires you to start making your own pop bonsai, my aim will be achieved.

Living plants need a lot of care, but they're definitely worth it. Hope to see you soon somewhere on the planet!

■ 撮影協力 Cooperation

アルファアイズ株式会社　ALFA EYES Co., Ltd.
株式会社アロハ・プロダクションズ　aloha productions
株式会社ビーサイド　B★side Co., Ltd.
オリオンビール株式会社　Orion Beer Co., Ltd.
株式会社ゾナルト アンド カンパニー　ZONART & Co., Ltd.

■ イラストレーション Illustrations

室谷雅子　Noriko Murotani

(英文版) POP BONSAI

2004年3月5日　第1刷発行

著　者　田嶋リサ
撮　影　大沢尚芳
翻　訳　カースティン・マカイヴァー
発行者　畑野文夫
発行所　講談社インターナショナル株式会社
〒112-8652　東京都文京区音羽 1-17-14
電話　03-3944-6493（編集部）
03-3944-6492（営業部・業務部）
ホームページ　www.kodansha-intl.co.jp

印刷・製本所　大日本印刷株式会社

Printed in Japan
ISBN4-7700-2980-2